THE CIVIL WAR
SLAVERY

BY JIM OLLHOFF

VISIT US AT
WWW.ABDOPUBLISHING.COM

Published by ABDO Publishing Company, PO Box 398166, Minneapolis, MN 55439.
Copyright ©2012 by Abdo Consulting Group, Inc. International copyrights reserved in all
countries. No part of this book may be reproduced in any form without written permission from
the publisher. ABDO & Daughters™ is a trademark and logo of ABDO Publishing Company.

Printed in the United States of America, North Mankato, Minnesota.
122011
012012

 PRINTED ON RECYCLED PAPER

Editor: John Hamilton
Graphic Design: Sue Hamilton
Cover Design: Neil Klinepier
Cover Photo: Corbis
Interior Photos and Illustrations: AP-pg 10 (top); Corbis-pgs 4-5 & 19 (inset); Getty-pgs 8-9;
Granger Collection-pgs 6-7, 13-15, 17 (inset), 18, 19, 21, 23, 24-25 & 27; Joseph T. Zealy-pg 1;
Library of Congress-pgs 10 (bottom), 12 (inset), 20, 26 (top), 28, 29 & 32; Thinkstock-pgs 11,
12, 16-17, 19 (background) & 31.

ABDO Booklinks
To learn more about the Civil War, visit ABDO Publishing Company online. Web sites about
the Civil War are featured on our Book Links pages. These links are routinely monitored and
updated to provide the most current information available. Web site: www.abdopublishing.com

Library of Congress Cataloging-in-Publication Data

Ollhoff, Jim, 1959-
  The Civil War : slavery / Jim Ollhoff.
    p. cm. -- (The Civil War)
  Includes index.
  ISBN 978-1-61783-276-5
  1. Slavery--United States--History--19th century--Juvenile literature. 2. Antislavery
movements--United States--History--19th century--Juvenile literature. 3. United States--
History--Civil War, 1861-1865--Causes--Juvenile literature. I. Title. II. Title: Slavery.
  E449.O46 2012
  973.7'112--dc23
                          2011038348

CONTENTS

A NATION DIVIDED

The war between the North and the South had many names. In late 1860 and early 1861, several Southern states declared they were no longer part of the United States. Northerners called it "the war of the rebellion." Southerners called it "the war of Northern aggression." Today, the Civil War is known as the bloodiest four years in American history.

Battles raged in more than 10,000 places around the United States. About three million men fought in the war. More than 600,000 died, about two percent of the country's population.

And yet, for all the horrors of the Civil War, those four bloody years shaped the young nation. Slavery was finally stopped. The leadership of Abraham Lincoln and the military genius of Robert E. Lee became legendary. The war shaped the society and economy of the United States for decades to come.

Slavery was finally stopped during the Civil War years.

5

STATES' RIGHTS

There were many economic differences between the Northern and Southern states. The North had much more industry and business. There were steel factories, manufacturing facilities, and much more railroad development. More people lived in cities. In the South, more people lived in rural areas, on large farms called plantations. Cotton was the primary crop in the South.

Taxes were not always applied equally in the North and South. The South sometimes paid more for goods going to and from other countries.

States' rights—the amount of independence the individual states were allowed—was one of the big issues that split the North and South. The North was more comfortable with a strong central government, based in Washington, D.C. But the South wanted individual states to have more rights. The South wanted to limit the power of the federal government.

As the population of the North grew, it became more politically powerful. Southern slave owners were rich and influential, and were often elected to Congress. But they were afraid the North would gain more and more power. Tension between North and South spilled over into Congress, where actual fistfights broke out between lawmakers.

On May 22, 1856, South Carolina Congressman Preston Brooks attacked Senator Charles Sumner on the floor of the U.S. Senate. Two days earlier, Sumner had given an anti-slavery speech, and verbally attacked a slave owner related to Brooks.

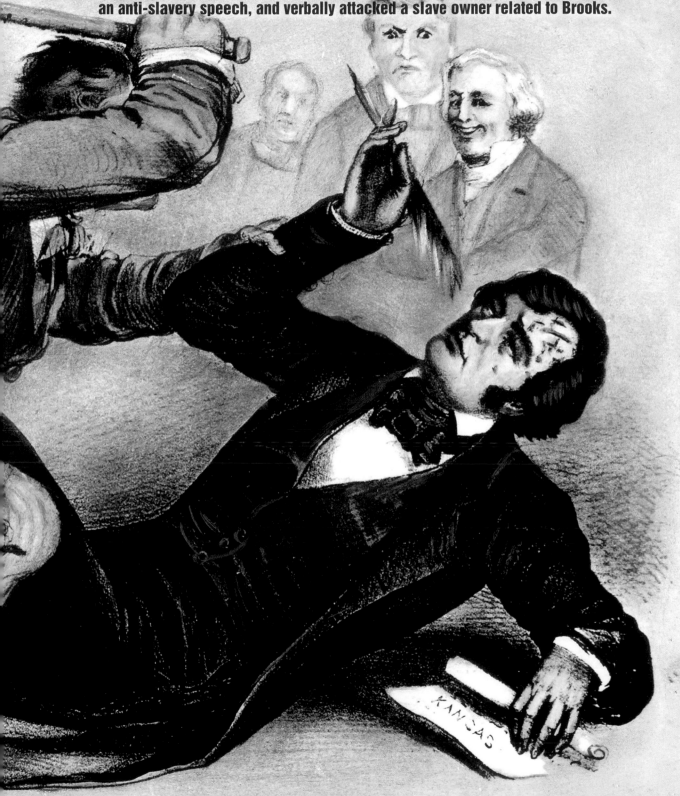

THE BONDS OF SLAVERY

There were many issues that separated the North and South, but nothing inflamed the passions of both sides like the issue of slavery. Slavery was an old institution, as old as human history. In the beginning, slaves were often people of a conquered nation. However, starting in the 1400s, European nations began to kidnap people from Africa. They were shipped to Europe and enslaved. Soon, slaves were captured because of their skin color, not because they were from a conquered enemy nation.

Slavery began in North America within 10 years after Columbus landed in the West Indies. Slaves were brought to the Caribbean Islands to work on sugar plantations. By the time the Pilgrims landed on Plymouth Rock in 1620, there were already 300,000 African slaves in the New World, mostly in Brazil, Mexico, and the Caribbean Islands.

Slaves harvest sugar cane on a plantation in the Caribbean.

A sculpture showing how slaves were cruelly transported on ships.

The Civil War began as a question of whether to preserve states' rights or whether to preserve the union of all the states. But more and more, it became a fight over slavery. One of the great leaders of the time, Frederick Douglass, was himself a former slave. He kept reminding people that this was a fight over human dignity and freedom.

Before the war, a small group of people opposed slavery because it was morally wrong. These people were called abolitionists. This movement, mostly in the Northern states, grew rapidly and became a loud voice for change.

Slaves were abducted from African kingdoms and transported in overcrowded ships to the New World. Many died on the trip across the Atlantic Ocean. When they arrived in North America, they were sold as if they were property. Families were ripped apart, taken in chains to different plantations around the region.

Slaves were forced to labor on plantations from sunrise to sunset. They were fed little and treated harshly. They were often whipped for no reason other than to remind them not to try to escape.

Frederick Douglass

Slaves of all ages worked picking cotton on plantations.

WHY DID THE SOUTH WANT SLAVERY?

The economy of the South was based largely on cotton. Raising cotton was very labor intensive and time consuming. Seeds had to be separated from the fiber. The fiber was then sold to textile mills to make clothes, blankets, or other products.

In the 1790s, American inventor Eli Whitney created the Cotton Engine, or cotton gin. This was a machine that separated the seeds from the fiber mechanically. Processing cotton became much quicker and easier, and the amount of cotton that could be grown and sold greatly increased. Landowners all over the South began growing cotton because it was a quick way to get rich. They needed people to work in their fields, and for that labor they needed more and more slaves.

Eli Whitney

Plantation owners supervise slaves operating an early hand-cranked cotton gin. The cotton gin separated the seeds from the cotton fiber, a task formerly done by hand. Processing cotton was suddenly quick and easy.

By 1860, the South was the world's leading producer of cotton. One out of every seven people in the South was a slave. Most Southerners didn't own slaves. But slave owners were rich and influential, often with hundreds of slaves. Many of these rich landowners were elected to Congress.

The Northern states were more industrial than the Southern states. Factory owners wanted cheap labor, just like on the Southern plantations. However, people from Europe who came to the United States usually landed in Northern ports. These immigrants, treated poorly and underpaid, provided cheap labor for the factories. The North didn't need slaves.

The abolition movement called for slavery to be stopped. One by one, most of the Northern states passed laws that abolished slavery. The Southern states braced themselves for a national fight to preserve slavery.

On December 3, 1860, Frederick Douglass (red vest) spoke at an abolitionist meeting at Tremont Temple in Boston, Massachusetts. His speech was disrupted by a mob of pro-slavery people accompanied by local police, who forced the abolitionists to leave.

In Congress in the 1850s, there were many bills that were introduced to end slavery. Some of the bills were motivated by a desire to end slavery because it was wrong. Other bills were motivated by a desire for political power. The bills inflamed passions in both the North and the South. Southern leaders were sure that abolition of slavery would cause economic ruin. And they were willing to go to war to preserve their economy.

THE MISSOURI COMPROMISE

By the early 1820s, some states allowed slave labor, while other states made slavery illegal. The South feared that if too many new free states (where slavery was illegal) joined the United States, then the free states would have more power in Congress. The South feared that if they lost slavery, they would face economic ruin.

One way to keep an uneasy peace was to make sure the number of slave states and free states remained about equal. When Maine and Missouri were considered for statehood, Congress agreed that Maine would join the Union as a free state in 1820, and Missouri as a slave state in 1821. This "Missouri Compromise" kept the balance equal between free and slave states.

With the 1849 discovery of gold in California, settlers and treasure-seekers poured into the territory. Talk of statehood began immediately. The North and South both wanted prosperous California to be on their side. In 1850, California joined the Union as a free state. Among people of the South, there was increased talk of leaving the United States— of declaring themselves to be a separate country.

FREE AND SLAVE AREAS
AFTER
THE MISSOURI COMPROMISE, 1820

Slaves helping their masters pan for gold in California territory in 1849. By 1850, California joined the Union as a free state.

17

SLAVERY IN LITERATURE

In 1852, a woman named Harriet Beecher Stowe wrote a novel called *Uncle Tom's Cabin*. It was a beautifully written novel, but portrayed the terrible cruelties of slavery. Its characters included Tom, the noble black slave, and Simon Legree, the greedy and brutal slave owner. The novel was a best seller, and it inflamed passions on both sides of the slavery issue. Northerners were horrified at the cruel treatment

Harriet Beecher Stowe

of black slaves portrayed in the book. Many people joined the ranks of the abolitionists, believing that slavery was morally wrong. Abolitionist newspapers grew in popularity. These newspapers reported about slavery, and encouraged people to fight against it any way they could. One of the leading anti-slavery newspapers was *The Liberator*. William Lloyd Garrison was the owner. His fiery writings helped give a voice to the anti-slavery forces.

William Lloyd Garrison published the anti-slavery newspaper called *The Liberator.*

THE DRED SCOTT DECISION

D red Scott was a slave living in Missouri. In the 1830s, he and his owner went to live in free areas, including Illinois and Minnesota. When the slave owner died, Dred Scott said that he was a free man, because he lived in a free state. His case went to court, and finally went to the Supreme Court of the United States.

In 1857, the Supreme Court decided against Dred Scott. They said that a slave could not be a citizen of the United States, and therefore, had no rights. In fact, the Supreme Court said that Congress could not restrict slavery anywhere.

Chief Justice Roger Taney handed down the Supreme Court's 1857 decision that stated slaves, including Dred Scott, could not be U.S. citizens and, therefore, had no rights.

Dred Scott and his wife and two daughters were freed by their owners less than three months after the Supreme Court's decision. Dred Scott died the following year, but his court case outraged people and made slavery a major political issue.

For several decades, there had been an uneasy peace between the slave states and free states. However, the Supreme Court decision outraged people in the North. People who had been undecided about the slavery issue suddenly became anti-slavery. Abolitionist voices swelled. Many state legislatures passed resolutions saying that they would not obey the Supreme Court's decisions.

There were many consequences of the Dred Scott decision. The most important consequence was that people wanted to elect a president who was anti-slavery. Abraham Lincoln was elected three years later.

FREDERICK DOUGLASS

One of the greatest leaders of the 1800s was Frederick Douglass. He was a former slave who escaped in 1838 and fled north. He became a tireless speaker for abolition and equality. He spoke for equal rights, not only for black people, but also women, Native Americans, and immigrants.

Douglass was a spellbinding speaker. He influenced and motivated people. When he spoke, people believed that he was the smartest person in the room. This was the opposite of the racist ideas of the slave owners, who said that slaves were ignorant.

Some people who heard Douglass speak were so impressed that they wondered if he could really have been a slave. Partly to answer those critics, Douglass wrote his life's story, *Narrative of the Life of Frederick Douglass, an American Slave.* It was published in 1845. This book gave people a clear look at the horrors of slavery. His writings and his work continued to push people to abolish slavery.

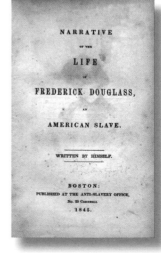

Frederick Douglass became friends with Abraham Lincoln. Douglass encouraged the president to create Union regiments of African Americans to fight in the Civil War. By the end of the war, nearly 200,000 African Americans served in the Union army.

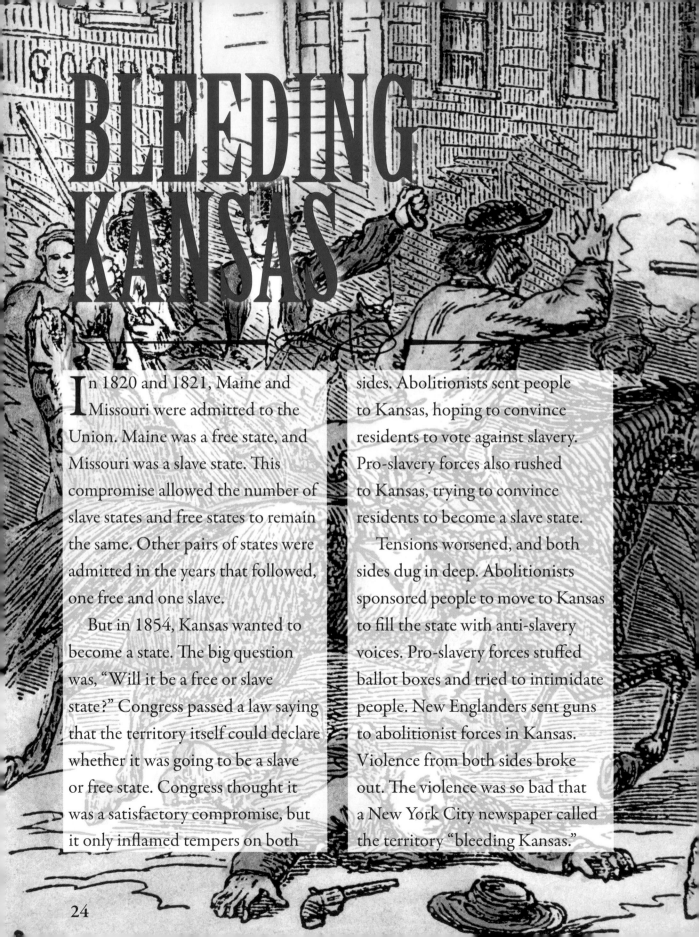

BLEEDING KANSAS

In 1820 and 1821, Maine and Missouri were admitted to the Union. Maine was a free state, and Missouri was a slave state. This compromise allowed the number of slave states and free states to remain the same. Other pairs of states were admitted in the years that followed, one free and one slave.

But in 1854, Kansas wanted to become a state. The big question was, "Will it be a free or slave state?" Congress passed a law saying that the territory itself could declare whether it was going to be a slave or free state. Congress thought it was a satisfactory compromise, but it only inflamed tempers on both sides. Abolitionists sent people to Kansas, hoping to convince residents to vote against slavery. Pro-slavery forces also rushed to Kansas, trying to convince residents to become a slave state.

Tensions worsened, and both sides dug in deep. Abolitionists sponsored people to move to Kansas to fill the state with anti-slavery voices. Pro-slavery forces stuffed ballot boxes and tried to intimidate people. New Englanders sent guns to abolitionist forces in Kansas. Violence from both sides broke out. The violence was so bad that a New York City newspaper called the territory "bleeding Kansas."

Pro-slavery forces attack the town of Lawrence, Kansas. The violence between abolitionists and pro-slavery forces in the 1850s caused the territory to be dubbed "bleeding Kansas."

JOHN BROWN'S RAID

Harpers Ferry, Virginia.

John Brown was a radical abolitionist who believed that violence was necessary to free the slaves. He spent time in Kansas with the abolitionist forces. In 1859, he organized 18 men to attack an arsenal—a fort where weapons and ammunition are stored. The arsenal was located in Harpers Ferry, Virginia.

On the night of October 16, 1859, he attacked and took over the arsenal. He believed that once he took over the arsenal, black slaves would flood to Harpers Ferry, and he could give them weapons and ammunition. This, he thought, would finally free the slaves.

However, no escaped slaves came to Harpers Ferry. The only people who came were a group of U.S. Marines, led by a colonel named Robert E. Lee.

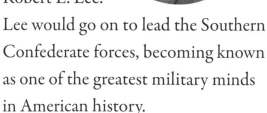

Robert E. Lee

Lee would go on to lead the Southern Confederate forces, becoming known as one of the greatest military minds in American history.

Lee and the Marines retook the arsenal, and John Brown was executed two weeks later.

John Brown violently opposed slavery. In the raid on Harpers Ferry, Brown's men killed four people. Ten of Brown's men were killed, including two of his sons. John Brown was captured and put on trial. He was found guilty of murder, conspiring with slaves, and treason against the state of Virginia. John Brown was hanged on December 2, 1859.

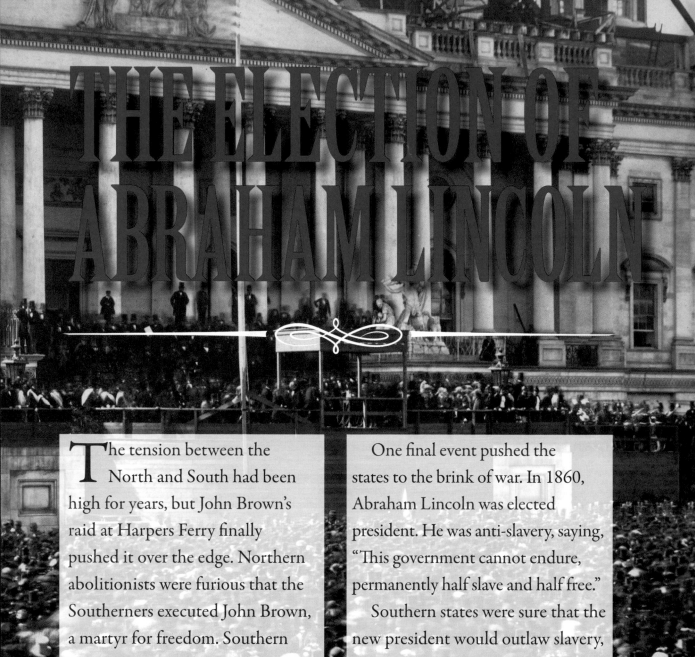

THE ELECTION OF ABRAHAM LINCOLN

The tension between the North and South had been high for years, but John Brown's raid at Harpers Ferry finally pushed it over the edge. Northern abolitionists were furious that the Southerners executed John Brown, a martyr for freedom. Southern pro-slavery forces believed that Northern abolitionists had sent the traitor John Brown to start a rebellion. Southerners worried that the slaves would rise up and murder them all. Both the North and the South began to organize military units.

One final event pushed the states to the brink of war. In 1860, Abraham Lincoln was elected president. He was anti-slavery, saying, "This government cannot endure, permanently half slave and half free."

Southern states were sure that the new president would outlaw slavery, which they believed would destroy their economy. It was the last straw. On December 20, 1860, South Carolina representatives voted to secede from the Union. Other Southern states followed shortly thereafter.

The Civil War was beginning.

Abraham Lincoln was sworn in as president on March 4, 1861. In his inaugural address he re-stated his oath to "preserve, protect, and defend" the government of the United States. The next month, on April 12, 1861, the Civil War began.

GLOSSARY

ABOLITIONISTS

Those who were anti-slavery, and believed that slavery was morally wrong.

ARSENAL

A fort where weapons and ammunition are stored.

CIVIL WAR

A war where two parts of the same nation fight against each other. The American Civil War was fought between Northern and Southern states from 1861–1865. The Southern states were for slavery. They wanted to start their own country. Northern states fought against slavery and a division of the country.

COTTON GIN

Short for Cotton Engine, a mechanical process for separating the cotton seeds from the fibers. The cotton gin was created by American inventor Eli Whitney in the 1790s.

IMMIGRANTS

People from other countries who come to live in America.

PLANTATION

A large farm where crops such as tobacco, sugar cane, and cotton are grown. Workers usually live right on the property. Early plantation owners in North America used cheap slave labor to make their operations more profitable.

SECEDE

To withdraw membership in a union or alliance.

UNCLE TOM'S CABIN

An 1852 novel by Harriet Beecher Stowe that described the horrors and injustices of slavery.

UNION

The Northern states united against the Confederacy. "Union" also refers to all of the states of the United States. President Lincoln wanted to preserve the Union, keeping the Northern and Southern states together.

An illustration from Harriet Beecher Stowe's novel Uncle Tom's Cabin.

INDEX